Winner of the L. E. Phillabaum Poetry Award for 2012

Mark Perlberg

THEATER
of MEMORY

new and selected poems

LOUISIANA STATE UNIVERSITY PRESS BATON ROUGE

Published by Louisiana State University Press
Copyright © 2012 by Anna Perlberg
All rights reserved
Manufactured in the United States of America
LSU Press Paperback Original

DESIGNER: Michelle A. Neustrom
TYPEFACE: Filosofia

Poems herein have been selected from *The Burning Field* (New York: William Morrow and Co., 1970); *The Feel of the Sun* (Athens, OH: Swallow Press/Ohio University Press, 1981); *The Impossible Toystore* (Baton Rouge: LSU Press, 2000); and *Waiting for the Alchemist* (Baton Rouge: LSU Press, 2009).

First publication of poems in these volumes appeared in journals as follows: *Hudson Review*: "The Floating World," "The Garden," "The Leap," "Lines for Some Landscapes of the Northern Sung," and "There Are Afternoons in Summer"; *The New Yorker*: "Hiroshige" and "The House Tree"; *Poetry*: "Garden Vision" and "When at Night"; *Prairie Schooner*: "At George Trambas' Body Shop," "The Box of Clouds," "The End of the Holidays," "The Island without Tourists," "The Kitchen Bird," "Nameless," "Nightsweat," "Orchids and Eagles," "The Passion of Vermeer," "A Question for Eugène Atget," "The Thought Garden," "Up in Maine," and "Waiting for the Alchemist."

Other poems appeared originally in the *American Scholar, Carleton Miscellany, Chelsea, Chicago Review, Chicago Tribune Magazine, Fifth Wednesday, Focus/Midwest, Free Lunch, Illinois Review, Images, Meridian, The Nation, Poetry East, Rhino, Today,* and *Willow Review*.

The new poem "Alexander's Castle" appeared in *Free Lunch*.

LIBRARY OF CONGRESS CATALOGING-IN-PUBLICATION DATA

Perlberg, Mark, 1929–2008.
  Theater of memory : new and selected poems / Mark Perlberg.
      p. cm.
  "LSU Press Paperback Original."
  ISBN 978-0-8071-4568-5 (pbk. : alk. paper) — ISBN 978-0-8071-4569-2 (pdf) —ISBN 978-0-8071-4570-8 (epub) — ISBN 978-0-8071-4571-5 (mobi)
  I. Title.
  PS3566.E6915T54 2012
  811'.54—dc23
                                                                                              2011051510

The paper in this book meets the guidelines for permanence and durability of the Committee on Production Guidelines for Book Longevity of the Council on Library Resources. ∞

Contents

FROM *The Burning Field* (1970)

    How the Summers Were 3
    The Indian Graveyard 6
    Buying Fish in Portland 7
    Dawn over Jewell Island 8
    How My Great-Uncle Louis Died Laughing 9
    Fred and Sadie Are Gone 10
    The Burning Field 11
    Hiroshige 14
    For a Dead Lady 16
    Stage Directions for an Unwritten Play 18
    Theology Lesson 19
    Prismatic 20
    To Katherine Eve 21
    The Moon Viewer 22
    Of Weightlessness 23
    The House Tree 24
    The Master Emil Nolde Paints *The Sailboat* 25

FROM *The Feel of the Sun* (1981)

    Baking Out 29
    Early One Morning 31
    There Are Afternoons in Summer 32
    Water and Light, Light and Water 33
    Bright Day on Lane Island 34
    In Praise of Lichen 35
    From Another Country 36
    Graffiti 37
    Seven Children: On a Photograph from Vietnam 38
    Poet to Poet 39
    Lonesomest Sound 40
    The Garden 41
    The Bewitched Mill 43

Lines for Some Landscapes of the Northern Sung 44
To T'ao Ch'ien from Vinalhaven, Maine 45
The Master 46
Three Translations of Classical Chinese Poems
    An Officer's Tartar Horse 47
    I Spend the Night in a Room by the River 48
    An Autumn Evening in the Mountains 49
Reflection 50
When at Night 51
The Leap 53
A Night Too Hot to Sleep 55
The Revenant 56

FROM *The Impossible Toystore* (2000)

In the Theater of Memory 59
Up in Maine 61
Coda 62
Bloodlines 63
Toward the Solstice 64
The Second Life of Christmas Trees 65
Pedagogy 66
Garden Vision 67
The Floating World 68
Love Letters 70
Half a World 71
Your Winter Coat 72
Alchemy 73
At a Holocaust Museum, Prague 74
Geode 75
Nightsweat 76
Self-Portrait: Camille Pissarro 77
Out There 78
The Passion of Vermeer 79
The End of the Holidays 80
From the Deep Kitchen 81
The Connubial Wrens 82

Maybe It Will Stir   83
Spaces   84
The Thought Garden   85
Return to the Island   86

FROM *Waiting for the Alchemist* (2009)

Silence at 5 A.M.   89
Orchids and Eagles   90
Waiting for the Alchemist   91
The Box of Clouds   92
Brothers   93
Once in a While   95
The Old Man in the Green House   96
The Dowser   97
In the Barbershop   98
At George Trambas' Body Shop   99
The Island Gift Shop   100
The Reading   101
My Muse   102
Your Dream, My Dream   103
Nameless   104
Song of the Platelets   105
A Late Birthday   108
More   109
A Question for Eugène Atget   110
In Memory of My Brother   111
The Island without Tourists   112
Against Cosmology   113
In My Next Life   114
The Revelation   115
The Kitchen Bird   116

NEW POEMS

The Mysteries of Hannah and Ivar   119
Poor Willy   122

For Jack and Natalie   123
Fresh Linen   124
Alexander's Castle   125
To a Helium Balloon Bought at the Zoo for Alex   126
An Afternoon with Bill Stafford   127
The Hidden Pool   128
The Beam   129
A Late Watercolor by Cézanne   130
At the Basil Leaf Café   131

AFTERWORD, *by Anna Nessy Perlberg*   133

FROM
The Burning Field
(1970)

How the Summers Were
to the memory of Fred Ramsdell

I was without a father,
but this tall man who had no children
helped ease that astonishing need,
for a few weeks of my boyhood summers,
better than I was able to understand
for twenty-five years.
And it may be that my turning up
at his big house on Casco Bay
filled a gap for Uncle Fred.
Perhaps as he snored beneath his wife's knitted comforter
he dreamed of sons.

However it was with Fred I cannot say,
but I do know that I followed him
everywhere about his place,
saying hello half-a-dozen times a day—
watching him paint his house white and yellow
on the bank above the bay,
standing tall on the painter's scaffold,
his ring of whitish hair
lifted by the wind.

I helped him water his lawns and his flower beds—
(his peonies and fat dahlias rocked heavily in the spray
as I turned their beds to mud)
and I went places with him that count with a boy
half-knowingly studying hard
to become a man.

Where did we go? Alone, in his old Dodge to the dumps
on the ocean side of the island;
downstairs to his white-washed cellar
where he kept nuts and nails and bolts in colored bottles,
and sharp tools that hung from the ceiling,
and (Hallelujah!) his outboard motor

that rested in a barrel of water from the tap.
How it bucked and splattered and smoked and roared
when he ran it in the barrel to run the ocean's salt out!

On Saturdays we went clamming with my sister.
We'd push off from the dock Fred built
with Captain Barker, once the master of the ferry.
We'd roar across the bay at the turn of the tide
to the flats on Diamond Island.
Fred's wife ran the lodge: we dug steamers
for the shore dinners she cooked
on Sundays.

—Once, the two of us knelt on his attic floor.
The spilled light of August warmed the beams,
while he worked to make a ring from the pit of a peach for me.
The floor was polished with age.
The sun went down as he ground the pit on emery.
But I cherish most a handful of Sunday evenings,
after the lobsters and the steamers
and the ball game we'd walk to in the center of the island.

Then he took my sister and me by the hand
to the drugstore on the corner: Richardson's it was called then,
and we sat, the three of us, cooling our inner arms
on the mottled marble of the counter.
Fans flapped: yellow flypaper turned slowly overhead.
"Two Uncle Fred Specials, please." He ordered.

I'm grateful for those men: Richardson in his straw hat,
the sleeves of his striped shirt
pushed back by elastic bands;
Uncle Fred in his speckled jacket,
with his speckled, peaked cap on.

The ball of ice cream floating in the pop poured from a bottle
was mighty special,
as was the lateness of the hour, with the sun gone,

and the dark flooding,
and the bugs that knocked at the street lamps
on our way home, as the stars came on.
But more special still were the voices of the young women,
talking on porches in their cotton dresses,
their arms and throats soft and glowing in the darkness,
as we walked home.

The Indian Graveyard

There was a place I had never been
but heard about from the older boys
on the island,
in hints and phrases of conversation
solemnly mentioned.

"There's an Indian graveyard
in the woods—I swear there is,"
one of them said,
"and the dead is buried,
not in the ground, but
in the tops of trees.

"Think of it when the night comes on,
when you lie in the dark,
and you say your prayers,

"Of all them Indians dead and gone
swaying forever in the air."

Buying Fish in Portland

Back on a busy wharf where seagulls
perch and turn, perch and turn,
two old men, the brothers Hamilton,
kept a fish store. What is it that draws me
to that quiet place, twenty years after?

Dim light, tall ceilings, the floorboards worn to gray
and sprinkled with sawdust that softened footfall,
and a cool efflorescence in those rooms
on a burning day in August,
and two old men standing behind the bins
where the sleek fish lay in billows of ice:
the great gray haddock and the cod
and the avocado-colored cusk—deep-diving, sweetest fish
in the blue Atlantic.

The brothers raised the zinc-covered lid
of the bin and pulled a fish out,
shaking off flakes of ice and slicing deep
into its flesh on the hardwood board—
then, into the scale, and then in the white
slick paper.

My stepfather was more himself
on those days, when he dressed in saddle shoes,
dared a snappy cap, and took his small stepson
by the hand for an adventure: To cross the bay on the steamer
to the quiet fish store in Portland.

The brisk air brought joy to him in the crossing.
On days such as those, and I am happy to remember,
he expected more from life.

Dawn over Jewell Island

The island lies like a sleeping animal on the horizon,
with black spears of pointed firs the length of its spine
and the dark thrust of an abandoned watchtower.
Above: cold crimson. Higher: rolling, slaty clouds
of the night's storm.
One listens for a shudder of drums.
The sun is alive (again) at the edge of the continent.

How My Great-Uncle Louis Died Laughing

My great-uncle Lou
died at eighty-three, or so,
in his rooms in the Sunset Cottage
that yellow-haired Polly,
ever the aspiring actress, ran.
He was killed by his own high spirits
and a nearly perfect poker hand,
or perhaps it was bridge.
Ah, superior exit—
and how in character for that old man:
whisked away while crowing with his companions
as the sun descended over Portland
and the cool summer night came on.

Across the street from the house
where ancient Uncle Lou died laughing,
other relatives and their tottering friends,
with faces painted strangely, and toad skins,
rocked on, on a dark porch.
There was beaked Florrie, with thin red hair
(Her white scalp showed in places)
and little Aunt Sarah—Brooklyn seamstress—
and the big woman who fell and broke her hip.
All dripped kisses, and I believe, love,
on a small, distant, visiting relative.
All had to wait for the common kind of death.

Fred and Sadie Are Gone

Fred and Sadie are gone.
The big yellow house standing above the bay
that sheltered so many summers—its rooms
scoured with clear air, with brimming sea light—
was sold by the bank to strangers.
Fred died first. Do his dahlias still rock
in June thunder?
In what tall grass is Tag,
Sadie's obstinate brown and white Persian, playing.

The Burning Field

Walked from the gray rock shore
where juniper and bayberry streak the air of summer,
through the woods toward the center of the island,
past stands of oak, past the gentle, shaking aspen,
then deep in the woods where the occasional birch
arches palely in green twilight across dark pine.
Suddenly, I came upon the abandoned baseball field.
The sun was high overhead.
Such a flood of light and silence poured from the clouds.

What a strange sight for gulls the field must make,
as they tack in the wind, straining their necks
with absolute animal seriousness
at the blank rectangular glare cut in the woods
where shade should flourish.
Perhaps it serves as a landmark for them
on their windy journeys above the islands,
above the bright bay flecked with boats.
Such a flood of brilliance pours up
out of the dark woods.

Tall grass burned to straw, and Queen Anne's lace
and dandelions waved across the outfield.
The base paths were cracked and narrowed,
the stands, bleached like driftwood to silver.

When I was a boy and came summer after summer
to this island, with its shore of rock and sand,
and its hills of green,
I walked on paths that led through the woods
to this field, where I watched the island team
play ball with men from other islands
down the bay.

Our team wore every kind of uniform, it seemed,
for those Sunday games, each man a living advertisement

with a label stitched across his back.
The shortstop played for the island and for Jones' Market.
The catcher pumped gas at Forest City Landing.

*Lay-deez and Gentlemen: The game today between Pine Island
and Cliff Island is about to commence. Pitchin'
for Pine Island: Thomas Gahagan. Catchin': Jim Gahagan.
At shortstop—*

Laughter, shouts, and a blur of sunbrowned arms and hands
and faces seemed held in the burning air,
and the field was a bright wave
in the heart of summer.

I would walk from those games a quarter-century ago
full of popcorn and soda,
and think of a time when Sunday girls
would follow me with narrowed eyes
and a catch in their breath
when I would be old enough to run
in such a field like the wind
and would stab the one in the ninth
that saved the game, before it crashed
into the pines.

I would follow the fat man
as he raised much dust at second base,
and also laughter.
(I learned not long ago that he
was asked to leave the island
because of some sad charge.)

And the orphan who raced in the outfield:
he peddled vegetables on weekdays, bumping
from house to house in a rusty truck.
(He was disinherited by his stepfather
for marrying a Roman Catholic.)

There was the man who ran the soft-drink stand
at the games. He sat beneath a canvas sunshade
and joked with the children.
(I am told that he was impotent,
so his wife took a lover into their house
and the three of them sat at breakfast.)

My friends, I have found that my own summer
with its sky-blue games has ended.
It was only half by chance that I came through the woods
to this place of easy victories and defeats.
So I lift my hat to you, who strode and leapt
and bucked across those high blue summer afternoons,
making me shout, or wince, or laugh as the game went.
I lift my hat to you, as I stand alone
in the burning field.

Hiroshige
Japanese woodblock print master (1797–1858)

Print, with his hand, his eye, was more than print,
and color more than color,
as the green of that Chinese vase—
cool as a brimming pond one thousand years—
as poem, paint, sound, or cut of stone
outglows its master.

That samurai is surely fast alive
in his hunched and silhouetted dozing, assback,
in the blur of fog, on the hump-backed
bridge.

      And the carved runners,
on my west wall, in a marvel of rain.
They slant into a shower of wind,
their burden heavy, the hill steep;
black tree-shadows leap behind the road.

Rain pleased this master, whether falling,
falling upon a dark, walled island keep,
or drenching beggar boys at play, or in sleep
in grasses by a baked summer road.
Their shriek, clear, echoes down my western hall.

Sun, wind, and star wined and pleased
him, in the prism of his largeness,
with his bags of color, on his sketching walks,
who rendered composed and perfect
a hawk's arc
above a distant snow-locked plain, star-stippled,
where men slept at the foot of frozen fires,
where perhaps one gray woman, at point
of earliest morning, squawked
cold talk of dreams to the frosty spirits of air.

But rising through the colors of his stories
(as a horseman approaching in forests of falling leaves)
the samurai moves; he rocks
in all odd angles in his doze,
past twin hanging towers of smoke
from anyone's embers,
past the seawall dripping water, and slow,
approaching with sleep in his eyes for a hundred years
the gate of stone, the lantern burning waxen,
and, in the hollow, the dream-hung,
the fog-blurred grave.

For a Dead Lady

for Marianne Hatch Wheeler, who died in Boston at thirty-four of pneumonia after giving birth to her third child

It occurred in a diminished time.
The city like a great brown bird
Shuddered in a snowless cold
As your windless afternoons unwound,
    aimless, slow as smoke,
Toward the birth of your final child.
       Then, on a day when snow
Whitened all the walks outside your hospital window,
And piled in the dark forks of trees,
Your fever climbed—climbed—
And turning toward the spreading warmth of a dream,
You died.

I do not know why your going touched me so,
That I again remember. I had met you only once.
Perhaps it is the snow
That whitens all the walks outside my window
And the fire that warms and reddens my room
On this hushed, other December.

I recall breasts that nosed like trout
In the waters of the evening's conversations;
That drowsed above your womb,
Taut with your final child,
And I recall the glow of polished hair
In an oval mirror
Above the curved back of a chair.

Yet why do I elaborate your death?
I had met you only once.

Is it the infant girl
Who was borne home to her nursery of shadows
Where her small sisters

Trailed across silent rooms
And stared and wondered and mourned?

Even for a stranger, my dear Nan,
That would be reason enough.

Or was it the doomed splendor of your youth,
That I knew I glimpsed, and again remember,
In the idle wander of your smile,
The shake of your head when you talked—
These seemed the lean, the pleading gestures of a stray,
Of one who once upon a distant Christmastime
Felt a gate swing shut in a wobbly Mother Goose rhyme,
And was lost.

Dear Nan, the child was already part of our world
As you lay, still cruising the snowy fields of anesthesia.
Then the rose of the fever flamed and you slid in the dark
Toward the cottage in the tall trees
Where firelight glowed in a low window.
The door opened as you approached; warmth flooded the fields,
And sweetly singing, lady,
You walked in.

Stage Directions for an Unwritten Play

>   (SCENE: A Manhattan park along the Hudson River viewed from an upper story. TIME: Early autumn.)

Sunlight moves above the river,
palest orange.

>   (Chords of music for the descending autumn sun)

In the park, chattering like spaniels,
children run.

The boy pulls a pink balloon that draws
the eyes of gulls circling the island,

and from my studio, the pink, poised four feet
above the grasses, pins the scene to its color.

>   (Chords of music for the harsh sun breaking behind the cliffs)

An Irish setter, his burn buttery,
glows upon the green. He walks his master,

while the sun, doing tricks,
drops fire in the window opposite,

where between two buildings
a turning shoal of pigeons silvers.

>   (And quiet music for the sleeping sun, preferably from an air by Mozart)

Theology Lesson

FIRST VOICE: But I cannot imagine eternity.
SECOND VOICE: Then think of what the sleeping rocks dream of.

Prismatic

Anything seems possible in a child's world.
A rain-wet plank
thrown on the ferny ground,
with a stick upright for steering,
becomes a car,
and, "Ouga! Ouga!" they go,
all six of them, all together,
banging into the heart of their game.
—The unanimity of it!
You'd think the six had one leaping mind
together.

But the sudden world of small children
is a world like the schizophrenic's:
it glints in fragments about them
from want of the simplest knowledge.
"Look," says Julie, "the trees are talking."
—But it was only birds.

To Katherine Eve

My child, I pray that your life
be as big and as fine and as round
as these meticulous arithmetic sums,
and that I, for my part, big bear,
may greatly help to give you
love and strength—also cunning
(and cunning that you will not use against yourself),
so that you will maintain
some of the same rough verve you wear
like your burly coat,
in which you barrel up the street
this February morning,
buttoned to the ears,
to your second grade.

The Moon Viewer

My daughter—fine hair falling
past the curve of her small cheek—
looks up from her crayon doodling
of squashed squares. She says,
"There's the moon, Mommie."
It rides like a bone in the clean morning sky.
"Your father knows a lot about the moon,"
her mother says, "and he'll teach you soon, when you get older."
The child replies, "How to catch it?"
Moons and squares rest in the blue silence
of her eyes.

Of Weightlessness

The fish in my aquarium
saunter in their element,
like lovers in a picture by Chagall.
They too ride airy, luminous,
above small, deserted villages,
enwrapped in the turning circle of themselves.
They have their own nosegays to nibble on, rest in, float upon,
as they glide in their fish tank wide and high,
with the unconcern of first lovers
for what dreams may flash through other watery skies.

The House Tree
a painting by Paul Klee

It is autumn, perhaps.
The tree that might still be covered with leaves
has grown three houses.

In a sky of smoky crimson a bird descends,
and moons and six-pointed stars
seem on the edge of appearing and disappearing.

A stick ladder leans against the tree
where a stick man poses,
doubtless before making the ascent.

Much is in motion, but when the stick man moves
in profile to start his climb,
the dream will dissolve like leaf smoke,
like a distant arpeggio,
and the dreamer will wake.

The Master Emil Nolde Paints *The Sailboat*

Like a great Chinese khan
you slap the paper with an ink-filled brush,
tilt it, drag the brush a bit
and an ocean appears.
The day on the paper is empty with fog:
there is no horizon at all.

You stroke the paper gently
there and here
and patches of space bloom . . .
Near the hint of birds turning,
in the slope of a wave,
between the sailboat that moves
out from your hand in obvious salt air
and the flaccid sea that now
lifts and slides.

FROM
The Feel of the Sun
(1981)

Baking Out
    Peaks Island, Maine

Old fellow, taking your ease by the hour in the sun
at the side of the clapboard house that faced the sea—
"baking out," you called it, and you sat still in the sun
half a day it seemed, head thrown back, eyes closed, smiling.
"My God, Harry, you're turning purple.
How can he sit so long in such a sun? Did anybody ever
see the like?" Mother was annoyed.
Such *sitzfleisch* made her angry.
"Where's Harry?"
"Where else? Baking out in the everlasting sun."
And on he sat in the summers turning dark
as the sun blazed its way across the sky.

What did he think about in the high hot sun of noon
and afternoon? I never thought to wonder—arrowing
off on errands of my own. But I wonder now:
Did he dream in the pummeling sun?
Did he listen as I do now (eyes closed, head thrown back)
for the rustle of wind like water foaming
high in the trees across the road,
for the scrape of bayberry in a great green clump near his chair,
to the noise of kids calling, of gulls cackling, heckling, cawing?
Did this random mesh of sounds please him?
—far from the East Side streets he knew as a boy,
far from the pummeling gangs.

"—Irish and Italians they were. They'd clobber you
if you left your territory and crossed into theirs.
(He recounted the threat with zest.)
I was short but could run like sixty.
Did I tell you the time I won a medal in track?
I was a city kid in a camp in the mountains.
I ran the hundred without track shoes. Track shoes?
Who ever heard of track shoes?"

It was the one glory exploit of his youth
I knew about. And the time, in a boys' club,
he sang in *The Mikado*.
"On a tree by a willow . . . ," accompanying himself
with fluting whistlings.

Did the scent of weed on the beach,
the minty breath of the fields please him,
as he purpled in the sun?
What of the sight of boats puttering, sailing, passing
on the endless lilting sea,
of birds hunting, drifting on rivers of air?

Mostly, it was the feel of the sun, I think,
my stepfather loved,
oiling the skin of the long dead boy,
pouring some kind of honey.
Maybe he stored it up in his chair on the lawn
so it would glow in him all winter,
through the fights, the arguments, the long subway rides,
the gray afternoons in the courthouse in the Bronx.

Old Harry, I hope that baking out
was your time to dream
long waking dreams bright as sails
in the late afternoon of your life,
dreams you let no one enter,
as you sat on your rented lawn
by the sea and the Maine islands
in the light of the man-eating sun.

Early One Morning

Until my walk this morning I had forgotten
that wind can be freighted with the scent of raspberries,

that things like ropes or an old pot on a porch
will creak in wind.

—A gull's shadow slides across the road,
ripples up the side of a house, and is gone.

There Are Afternoons in Summer

There are afternoons in summer that are so fine
they seem an interval of time's first day that has never ended
and will never end.

I am sure it is the palpable force of the light,
of light so clear that one sees everything open to air:
    the veins on the underside of leaves
    the sharp serrations of the fern
    the shadow cast by each small stone
    the glass edge of the sea that is the horizon's line
    the sun flinging diamond fires from a patch of the bay,
    the luminous wing-edge of a gull crossing.

The illusion dies as the day dies
when light lies down level in the weeds
and the sky in the west takes color like a bruise
and the evening walks in cold shadows like the morning.

Water and Light, Light and Water

1

At the lake's edge
in an inch of water
minnows move above sand ridges
stroked by loops, by nets of light.

2

The late sun hangs over the lake's rim.
Rings of light, shaken from the water,
climb the cedars.
Along the broken pier the clear light
sings in the thistles.

Bright Day on Lane Island

Small wind noises: puffs, hissings,
watery susurrations.
Tough plants erect in stony meadows:
raspberry, juniper, wildrose, goldenrod.
Old rock, gray-green, lichen-starred.
And pouring light everywhere flooding
this little island, the outer islands,
the great blue lyric sea.

In Praise of Lichen

It lives on mere banks and drifts of air
And where nothing else will,
Growing in ashy moonbursts on bare boulders
in the sun's brightest flare, beneath a shine of ice,
in blowing salt air.
Its medallions color the bark of trees;
They seal gravestones—a glad sign
In the windy margins of the world, of increase
Near the domain of zero.

From Another Country

The children have gone, leaving their round signs
and hieroglyphs—fragments of the language of their country—
chalked on this darkening asphalt edge of the park.
They have set down numbers, carefully, in a ring
(some are written backwards). And they have drawn dreamy girls,
each with a crescent smile and bouncy hair,
and crowned each head with a bow. The park is silent;
a leaf floats down to the chalky center of the scene.
But what matters is no longer in the picture:
The artists have scattered to their suppers and their baths,
leaving in the hour's tranquil light a sense of emptiness.
It is clear that those who worked with such seriousness here
were girls, but there is no hint of their individual lives,
for all the chalky drawings are the same.
So childhood was a gate through which we came.
Pharoah's children, too, must have sketched
just such marvelous matters upon perishable walls.

Graffiti

The most important part of Spaceship Earth: the instruction booklet that didn't come with the package.

Everybody wants to go to heaven but nobody wants to die.
—*Lincoln Park, Chicago*

How to put it briefer, better—
the cosmic grumble: I ache, therefore I am?
Your sayings, nameless calligraphers,
penny metaphysicians,
painted on rocks at the lake's edge
in colors that shine in rain!

Seven Children: On a Photograph from Vietnam

My daughters started home on a summer day
as clouds, blue with electricity, piled in the sky
and drops began to smack against the street.
When they turned the corner, lightning raveled the air,
thunder cracked, wind, rain lashed them.
Down the street they raced, screaming,
and fell in the door out of the storm,
wet as if they had been lifted by their mother
out of the tub, accusing.
Where was Father when the sky broke,
who had met them only at the door?
Pieces of that day still flicker in their dreams.

Now come five small children of Vietnam
running out of a photo in the news.
The white-shirted boy nearest bitterly shrieks/cries: fear
lives in his face.
A girl in the center, naked, holds out her arms,
hands dangling (as though flicking off bath water;
as though to be lifted by someone from the tub).
The jellied fire eats her narrow back.
An older girl bumps along the road
with a small boy. They hold hands, running.
And the littlest stops and looks behind him.
They are fleeing storms of fire, of tiger-roar/lion-roar,
of dragon crash and bellow.
What of their dreams, after the flesh of the burned girl
has stopped melting like wax into the napalm?
Father, whom will they accuse?

Poet to Poet

I know a poet—he wears dark glasses always,
even after nightfall.
His advice, a mountain-man's knowledge,
delivered in soft West Virginian:
"Don't let the bastards get a bead on ya."
Which I take to mean,
be elusive, like quicksilver rain,
be sudden as ground fog, and scary,
be not straight or plain; be hidden,
take the sly cat for totem.
Be nobody's pet.
Make Hermes your guide, patron of thieves,
winged wayfarer god with a fondness
for bent ways, for crossroads.
Be secret as a spy, various, patient,
and you'll get by.

Lonesomest Sound

What if all the sounds ever made
do not dissipate in space
but travel on and on like light from a star.
Somewhere over the land, the *whoo-whoo-ee*
of a scrapped diesel train. Lonesomest sound.
You who are old as I will hear it again,
hoarse above dream fields.

The Garden
in memory of my mother

For weeks you had been journeying into yourself,
slowly at first, and writing occasional poems
to mark certain junctions, dark and airy crossings.
Then as the illness gathered
and you began to shrink before our eyes,
like a figure disappearing in space,
your flight became a kind of inward freefall.
The last station you came to before the end was fear,

Fear so insistent that in your hospital room
above the city, now remote as Arcturus,
you lay in a white silence, entirely alone—the living
      who came to you refused to countenance your journey—
your face drawn about the bone, eyes uprolled, mouth gone,
contracted on a single point of terror.

It was your daughter who loosed you from that mooring
by naming names:
Out of her own teeming conversations with herself
she knew that one must agree to meet with the dying,
      under a favorite tree, out on the edge of town,
      in front of a rain-streaked shop,
and walk part way with them, touching hands.
At last you had found a pilot for your journey.
It was a dusky afternoon in deep August.
Shadows of leaves stirred on the walls of the room.

She told you, now an unfamiliar, small old lady,
that she knew you would be able to do it,
and she returned bright fables learned from you as a child.
She said it is like the seasons following one another,
She talked of seeds sailing,
of how the tall trees burn,
of swallows blowing about in a gusty sky.

She said there would be a garden
bright with so many flowers, with walks and grasses.
And your eyes widened at last before the end.
The great fear left you,
you grew easy in your pillows
and stepped light as a girl
into the banks of shadows
that now drowned the walls of the room.

The Bewitched Mill
a painting by Franz Marc

Water falls upon the great wheel,
and at the gathering pool beneath the mill
blue animals drink.
And birds on branches flash and sing
in the arch of falling water.

Some beasts have come to drink
that they may never die;
others to be whole again.
But some move out of the woods
toward the rumor of the dusky waters
so they will not forget, down the fall of years,
the possibility of exultation.

Lines for Some Landscapes of the Northern Sung

Walk on beside your oxen, atom of a man.
Can you hear the water threading the brown cliffs high and
    away?
It plunges down the mountain into cloud,
    doubtless the source of the amber stream at your feet.
We are on a journey, you and I.
Perhaps you will lodge tonight at the inn that casts no shadows,
    across the stream, and then proceed refreshed
To the dark temple whose peaks break through the crab-claw
    trees
Beyond the bridge,
Seeing only the next turn of the tricky path.
But I can set my spirit soaring like the wind, like a ninth
    Immortal,
Everywhere at once in Fan K'uan's mountains.
I can leap the cliffs sheer, listen for the wind moaning
    in the gorges—was that a gibbon's scream—
Float like mist in and about all the hollows,
While you clip-clop on, following your nose.
Never mind, we are both pilgrims in these tea-colored
    mountains
That pile into the crisp air with such vast solidity,
You by inheritance, I by hankering.
They tell us our place. They say something
Is solid as a planet in this heaving world.
And they say, perhaps, with T'ao Ch'ien,
That when the time comes for us to go into the mountains—
Do not make a fuss,
Step out quietly on the stream,
For the wind that blows against these peaks,
That shakes against the stars above the mountains,
Moves in your blood, and you and I are shadow and star.

To T'ao Ch'ien from Vinalhaven, Maine

What would my old friend say of this prospect,
who, from a bird's homeward flight,
from the sight of sun lingering on Southern Mountain,
"almost learned the truth."

You are beside me here, T'ao Ch'ien.
Tell me, what do you think of the mist
erasing that jagged row of pines
descending the slope to the bay?
Does not the scene recall a Chinese painting?
I think you'd admire the road, the green, the snail
glistening with wet,
and berries—drops of blood-red jade—
just off the path in the woods,
and scent of mint and dogrose blowing.

Today I climbed the hill to the island graveyard
and lay in the grass to read
the lichen-spotted stones.
One took my heart, Old Ghost,
not twelve inches high—"Lottie,
dau. of G. & A. F. Young, born 1883,"
dead nine years later.
"This is a little grave, but O, have a care,
For world-wide hopes lie buried here.
How much light, how much joy
Lies buried with our darling girl."
Lilies and the morning glory—carved
in the sea-gray stone.

Master, let us converse and make what we can
of all these things.
We'll meet at the eastern hedge.
Let me bring the wine you were so fond of.

The Master

Near the edge of a town on the River Wei,
where a few scattered huts climbed the back of the mountain,
lived one so schooled in the tao of painting,
his curling dragons flapped off walls.
They raced storm clouds and entered
the watery life of streams.
Near Ch'ang-an was another: a silk wind moved
    in his bamboo groves.
Spring, like memory, stirred in a room
where his pictures hung.
But what do you make of the master of masters
(he was seen at odd hours on the streets of the capital)
who, tiring of the world of men,
painted a cave and disappeared inside.

Three Translations of Classical Chinese Poems

AN OFFICER'S TARTAR HORSE
 by Tu Fu

This is one of the Tartar horses of Ferghana.
Note its great frame, so lean, so angular.
Its ears rise up like pointed bamboo shoots.
Its hoofs are light as wind.
To a beast with such esprit
I could trust my life. With such a horse,
for whom ten thousand miles is a morning gallop,
I could face eternity.

I SPEND THE NIGHT IN A ROOM BY THE RIVER
by Tu Fu

Darkness still shadows the mountain road
as I gaze from my study above the watergate.
Streamers of cloud rest on the brow of a cliff,
while the orphan moon tumbles among the waves.
A line of cranes winds overhead in silent flight.
Below, a pack of wolves quarrels over food.
Grieved by the war, I have not slept.
Who has the strength to right heaven and earth?

AN AUTUMN EVENING IN THE MOUNTAINS
by Wang Wei

A fresh rain in the empty mountains
has brought with it the chill of autumn.
The clear stream flows over rocks and pebbles.
Water lilies shake beneath a passing fisherman's boat.
From the bamboo grove—the chatter of girls
returning with their wash.
The fragrance of spring has run its course,
but you, old friend, stay with me a while.

Reflection

Hands in a night window
I thought meant harm—
my own.

When at Night

My father sleeps in the sun porch
on a strange white bed.
I know what *gestorben* means.
Nobody said.

One day my father picked me up.
Ach du lieber Augustin, he sang, he sang.
Around, around the living room,
the big house rang.

He loves my sister more.
Sister's small and fat.
When I grow up I'll be like him—
gold mustache and a straw hat.

What does dying mean?
Is it living like a stone?
Being everywhere at once,
like river mist or rain?

Mama cries and cries.
She's wearing out her eyes.
Be a big boy, a good boy.
I don't cry.

In Mr. Gumbie's yard
the trees are clipped and strange;
the branches wrapped in gunny sacks
like bandaged hands.

Gumbie's in a box.
I saw, across the way.
They put the lid on.
They took him in the rain.

His face was brown as leaves.
He was bent and sick,
inching past my window,
loose coat, tapping stick.

I dream about my father.
Wind and cold rain.
He doesn't have a face.
The wind blew away his name.

The Leap

My family moved to Kansas when I was a girl.
Father was an engineer and worked on a project there.
We lived in a house beyond the edge of town;
It stood by itself at the foot of a long, sloping hill.
Mother was strict. Every afternoon, even in summer,
She'd come to where I would be playing alone
And say, "Lou-Ann, go upstairs now and take your nap. It's
    time."
So, after a time I'd drag off with my doll to my room
Near the attic; it looked out over the wide empty fields.
Well, summers in Kansas are just not to be borne.
The heat goes over a hundred in the fields
And in any room in a house where the sun falls.
I was just a child; I couldn't stay on my bed,
    it got so warm.
I would lie on the floor with a cool patch of boards
Against my back, and smell the dust in my room,
And listen for the heat crackling in the empty fields.
Then, after a while, I'd get up and look out my window—
    way up the hill. And every afternoon at three
She'd come. Oh, it wasn't my mother.
A lady would ride up the hill on a great white horse.
She was dressed in white, always.
She'd rein in her horse at the brow of the hill
And stand there, looking.
Then she'd leap—horse and all—into the river.
I learned to wait for her ride in that sullen heat,
Every day at three in the afternoon,
And for her long silent fall to the water.

I kept that story to myself for thirty years.
Then one day I told Mother.
"Lou-Ann," she said, "I'm amazed.
You know there wasn't a river near our house.
The nearest was twenty miles away."

"Is that so," I said. "Isn't it strange, then,
that I learned to wait for the woman and her white horse,
that I counted on their coming,
and their leap together—their long floating fall to the river—
all those summer afternoons,
in the heat, in my room,
in the house in Kansas."

A Night Too Hot to Sleep

One night long ago
on a night as dank as this,
my father came to our room.
"How would you and Sis
like to go out for a ride?
It's much too hot to sleep."

I recall my sister's face
upturned to greet his
as he carried us downstairs,
how her hair bobbed up and down,
and the ribbon in her hair.
And even the shift she wore,
dotted with little bears.

We stepped out into the night
out of the square of light
that fell from the front door
and got in the big car
and rode around the town
with our father.

So great a treat it was,
so rare a treat it was,
it lingers with me still:
the three of us in the car
tooling around the town
on a night too hot to sleep.

My father was soon dead.
Of his few nights with us,
this is the one I keep.

The Revenant

I came, a stranger, an intruder.
I arrived from long ago
and on a fur-soft summer night
parked my car in tall shadows
that half-hid the house my father built.
It rose in the darkness, still commanding the street
at the head of the hill where the cliffs and the river meet.

A young man came down the slate walk
where I played as a child,
when June evenings were stitched with fireflies.
He stood outside the hedges.
"Can I help you, sir?"
"Thank you," I said. "No—but I used to live here once."
"Oh," he said, then turned and walked briskly into the dark.
No ghosts for him this evening.

I might have said, but had sought to spare us both,
that my father, when he was younger than I am now,
had built this house, and died suddenly after,
on the porch that faces south.

What had I hoped to find in this mute return—
that my unknown parent had inherited his house in death?
That he was the true tenant, still there
in the shrubs, the garden, the insubstantial air;
did I expect to hear his laugh, to feel his hand upon my hair?

Who now was the ghost, my father or myself,
who like a stone fallen out of space,
had struck across the orbit of this young man,
raising I cannot know what dust
in the cliffs and precipices of his mind.

FROM
The Impossible Toystore
(2000)

In the Theater of Memory

I think of the time I entered
the toy shop with you
on an afternoon gray with the threat of rain.
Or do I recall images of you reminiscing,
recounting the story you loved to tell
of your small stepson-to-be
standing mute before racks, tables,
shelves of toys?

You would have purchased any of them
for me—lead soldiers firing muskets,
a mountain tunnel for my trains,
even a magic cape sewn with planets and stars—
but I never pulled my hands
from my pockets.

What I recall clearly is the way
you shook your head with mirthless laughter
each time you told the story down the years
of the strange boy who turned his back
on a hundred toys.

Only months before we entered the impossible
toystore, my father quit the family
by performing the unfathomable trick of dying.
Surely, he could have reversed the magic
that engrossed him as he lay on his bed
in the darkened room.
Surely, he could have turned the key
in the lock of himself and slipped the chains
he chose to wear, like Houdini,
another prince of the time.

Was not the story you never tired of telling
a slant account of a vexed and baffled boy

who would not forgive his father for disappearing,
nor you, your entrance on the scene?

For I had seen him glide from our home
on a June evening,
saw him lift his straw boater in the air,
flash his broad Franklin Roosevelt smile,
then turn and vault the hedge
at the border of the lawn.

His heels made sidewalk music
down the street.

Up in Maine

Mother drew me toward her
on the lawn, kneeled,
and took my hand.
"You must call Harry—Father—now.
Will you do that for me?"

I pulled my hand from hers
and walked away.

I see her kneeling on the grass,
white arms at her sides.
She turns and looks
out toward the bay.

Coda
for my mother

When I was six or seven
you stopped singing
as you moved about the house
as you dressed for evening

I'll see you again whenever
spring breaks through again
Time will lie heavy between

Remember the night

You played the piano
a piece with vivid Spanish
figures

I recall the fringed peach shawl
on the polished mahogany
When did you learn to play
You must have spent hours practicing
Why did you stop singing

If I had thought to ask
these questions when I was older
could you have found a way
to answer

Bloodlines

On the back of an old photograph of you
I found four words you wrote;
they noted merely place and time.

Mother, that sudden token of your writing—
angular pitch of urgent, sloping letters—
blew wide the door to the country
we loved and warred in. Your sign.
solid as a thumbprint, a gene map.
Never to appear anywhere in the world
again.

Toward the Solstice

We burned our leaves on the bluest October day,
the sun still warm on our backs,
frost just a ghost in the shrubbery.
We raked the leaves into shifting piles on the lawn,
scooped them into deep round baskets
and spilled them in the street against the curb.
The vein of fire, unseen at first in diamond light,
whispered through oak leaves brown as butcher paper,
and maple still flushed with color like maps
torn from *The Book of Knowledge*.
We were letting go of October, relinquishing color,
readying ourselves for streets lacquered with ice,
the town closed like a walnut, locked inside the cold.

The Second Life of Christmas Trees

In frozen January, my friends and I
would drag discarded Christmas trees
from the sidewalks of our shivering town
to an empty lot. One match and fire
raced down a dry sprig like a spurt of life.
A puff of wind and the pile ignited,
flamed above our heads. Silk waves.
Spice of pitch and balsam in our nostrils.

We stood in a ring around the body of the fire—
drawn close as each boy dared,
our faces stinging from the heat and cold,
lash of that wild starburst on a winter night.

Pedagogy

My first-grade teacher, Pearl Lorraine Wright,
stood before her class, her hair a thin,
fleecy cloud.
"Children, it's not good for your eyes
to wear rubbers all day in school.
Put them in the cloakroom, please."
Even then I smiled behind my hand.

"Children, watch me. This is how to
open a new book without cracking
the spine."

I settle in my study, out of a whirling
storm, snap on the gooseneck lamp,
and open a new book, *Dawn of Art:
Paintings from the Chauvet Cave*,
set the spine on the desk,
press the boards down and smooth out
the pages, a few at a time, half right,
half left, and think of Miss Wright,
in Palisade School Number 4,
in a town that no longer exists.
Bisons, horses, rhinos, lions
march across the golden wall
of the cave—my snow boots neatly
placed in the hall closet.

Garden Vision
after the painting by Paul Klee

It is a soft night on the streets of my city
with gold October burning in the air.
The sky is palpable, smoky,
remote from the glass-hard sky of winter.
We have been given Rilke's two more golden days.
It is time to wander after work under rustling leaves,
saffron streetlights, toward my autumn garden.
It will appear at a turn of some unlikely street.
Maybe there will be a stream, beyond a patch of thistles
patterned with leaves,
a stone path worn smooth by desire,
a shell of a tower, each brick burning within
like the yellow flares of the leaves,
a sun dial, its blade sheathed in the dark,
a pumpkin moon glowing like a heart,
and at the far end of my garden,
a wall etched with signals and runes
that will tremble as I read them
into meaning.

The Floating World
  for Anna

1

Sounds of koto and flute spool from the radio
this January morning.
Thirty years ago we were in Japan.

2

Fuji's snow-cone, flushed in early light,
soared above the gate at the edge of the garden,
as though we'd borrowed the holy mountain—
visible from a hundred miles away
only in clearest air of winter—for the morning.
When we rose my shirt was so cold you thawed
it at the stove. I left the house,
turned a corner,
and the mountain disappeared.

3

Blowing curtains in the wine shops.
Fire in the waxed-paper lanterns
red as blood.

4

Returned to our room in the 300-year-old inn,
its walls, sliding doors, brown as oak leaves.
In the light of the floor lamp, our futon spread
to receive us was the color of moss in noon sunlight.
Rain brushed the city, dripped
from the evergreens, the stone lantern
in our private garden.

5

You sang lieder with our student-guide in Kyoto
eight years after Hiroshima.
Temples, palaces, a walled sand garden.
Back home, I failed to answer his letter.

6

These scenes from the beginning of our story
shine like slides on a white wall.
I reach for them, give them the permanence
of thin lines of ink on ruled paper.

Love Letters

Our letters you packed so long ago
in the transparent plastic box—
Plastics were new then.
The box seemed quaint a decade later
when plastics no simple saw could cut
or fire burn entered all our lives.
You tied our letters into packets,
dropped them into the brittle case
that had, itself, to be tied with string.

The many times I said, "Burn the letters.
Feed them to some small, inconsequential flame."
Too late, after the crash that took us
like a pair of storm-smashed birds.

I didn't want our children rummaging in our letters.
The things we told each other—sundered
by the usual, useless war. I didn't want them
reading wild words about the meadow your body
was to me. Its shoreless stream.

Burn the letters? As usual you were wiser.
They will sift through them one by one.
Children, we were shameless.
Flameless the fire in which we burned.

Half a World

At the zoo in a microsecond
you were left
with a single good green eye.
Quick as a bird passing
a shadow bloomed
deep behind the lens
of the other.

Now I wake before dawn and listen
for your small night noises.

Should we imagine our world halved
by the absence of the other—
in form of inoculation—like the king
who supped each day on a drop of poison
and died old?

Your Winter Coat

Remember that winter coat
I was so fond of?
We picked it out together
at the beginning of our story.
Threads of isfahan red close-woven
with nubby strands of black. Silk-soft.
I loved helping you unbutton
its long row of small black buttons
when you came in from the cold.

Last night it shone
like a Persian carpet in a sunny room.
I woke with tears on my face.

Alchemy

Kafka lived in this small blue house
that teeters and leans on Alchemy Street,
where Emperor Rudolph installed scholars
to coax tin into gold. It's just a shout
from the castle of a thousand rooms.

"I'll ennoble the man who brews gold in a pot,"
the emperor said.

"The castle," said Kafka, "that we see
from every point in Golden Prague
is a swarm of shadows. It isn't there.
I've tested its reality with alchemical
instruments of my own. It's built
entirely, stone on stone, of air."

At a Holocaust Museum, Prague

In the photomural a boy of twelve looms
in a crowd beside the transports.
He wears a sweater buttoned to the throat
against the chill, hefts a suitcase
as though leaving with his family on a holiday.
Big shoulders, chest, hair fresh-cut,
alert strong face that fell to ash,
melted in smoke, in ropes and sheets of snow
flying over Poland.
Decades later, in another country,
my brother wore that face.

Geode

I had a friend who imperceptibly
became my bitter foe.
I don't know which the more painful,
the poison drop by drop,
or the shock of the turning
that grew unknown to him or me
like crystal teeth inside a stone.

Nightsweat

The poem I need to write is the poem of rage.
Not the poem of sinking into harmony with wind rhythms,
wave sounds lapping this northern island.
Nor the poem of the round of seasons, effulgent summer
dying into fall. Nor of taking my place
in the cycle of generations.

I need to write how the great wind came on a filthy night,
rammed up the coast, ripped spruce eighty feet tall
and strewed them like straw over a neighbor's
woodlot, a man who built his house deep in those woods
and painted it black.

I need to write of the squire on the crest of my hill,
who left a trail of stumps and ash from his house
clear down to the bay, trashing a woman's land
because her treetops smudged his view of sunsets,
clouds, boats passing.

How my daughters, both, were given
halting, difficult sons.
Of their nightsweats, vigils, sorrows.
But most—how the surgeon split my chest
with a whirling saw and took out my heart.

O blooming world of chaos and decay,
I want my old heart back, not this alien pump
that was pressed, cut, chilled, changed,
and held in hands remote from me
as those of a man on a spacewalk, working
with delicate instruments
in the violent dark.

Self-Portrait: Camille Pissarro

He stares at me like my conscience,
looming before a window open on a street
in Paris. His life is almost over.
He says: This is who I am.

All is dark and silvery. The fall
of his beard, light glinting on a rim
of his half-glasses. The window silvery behind him.
He says: The world doesn't flow in circus colors.
That vision isn't serious. It moves in plainer
shades: browns, greens, cloud colors,
and this buoyant, silvery light of Paris.

He says: I prefer what happens again and again.
Peasants in a row mowing. Patterns of movement
on the boulevards, shifting yet the same.
A farm girl in a violet dress,
head awkwardly bent, musing over her bowl of coffee.

Out There

The Chinese painters didn't use
a vanishing point to show perspective.
Washes of light and lighter color
indicated distances—past cliffs, streams
and humped bridges, past water falling
from the lip of a rock into a gorge,
out to farthest pales and shallows,
where the Immortals ride great fishes and turtles,
sporting in the unseen world.

The Passion of Vermeer

Whether a servant girl is pouring cream into a bowl,
or a young woman, elegant in satin, glances
in a mirror at her knight as she plays the clavier;
whether the turbaned girl, grown famous
these three hundred years, looks suddenly back
at the viewer, lips parted,
the subject of the painter was time—
seized by fixing what is most fleeting.

That is how it was, you say, and is,
as your wife plays an old tune on the piano,
as sunlight streams across your desk,
striking the road atlas open for a trip
and the photo of your son balancing
on one leg beside a gate, smiling.

The End of the Holidays

We drop you at O'Hare with your young husband,
two slim figures under paradoxical signs:
United and Departures. The season's perfect oxymoron.
Dawn is a rumor, the wind bites, but there are things
fathers still can do for daughters.
Off you go looking tired and New Wave
under the airport's aquarium lights,
with your Coleman cooler and new, long coat,
something to wear to the office and to parties
where down jackets are not de rigueur.
Last week winter bared its teeth.
I think of summer and how the veins in a leaf
come together and divide
come together and divide.
That's how it is with us now
as you fly west toward your thirties.
I set my new cap at a nautical angle, shift
baggage I know I'll carry with me always
to a nether hatch where it can do only small harm,
haul up fresh sail and point my craft
toward the punctual sunrise.

From the Deep Kitchen

Fill a large pot with cold water.
Add chunks of celery, parsley root,
and the purple-tinged turnip.
When the vegetables soften,
slide the chicken into the pot.
When the bird is golden, add sprigs
of parsley and carrot circles.
The yellow broth will soothe you.
The meat steeped in the liquor
of root vegetables will sustain you.
This is the message from the deep kitchen
of childhood. Pass it on.

The Connubial Wrens

Yes to the golden moment that is gold
a moment only in the cramped dirt garden
in our back yard. Yes to the tottering wall,
the blunt back porches of anonymous neighbors,
the toys abandoned on flagstones—
yellow tractor, dump truck, chunky cement mixer.
Yes to the crows in their baseball umpire suits
on the telephone wires, to the connubial wrens
hunkering in the Chinese elm, its leaves still green.
Yes to the black squirrel eyeing me
from the gate, the herbs in their pots,
sage, thyme, sweet marjoram,
the jet flashing this instant overhead.

Maybe It Will Stir

He moves now at the edges of the world
in windy margins where sleet spills into rain,
where the sea flows into the mouths of northern rivers.
He listens for what might be in wind-ripples, indications,
watching how dusk, issuing its purple,
takes a far-off hill.
He's grown used to fingering silence,
like a merchant his coin.
Maybe it will stir in the shadow of stones,
in a trumpet note of light glancing off a wave.

Spaces

Leave a space for the unexpected.
The red sun put out by fog at noon.

The tree backlit on our walk that night—
a vast face on the fog's scrim.

The adagio of Mahler's Fifth on the radio
when we came in, played not like a dirge
but a song.

The Thought Garden

I will build a thought garden behind my house.
Raked sand or gravel flowing will stand
for a stream, the sea, or trackless woods.
Gnarled rocks anchored in twos, threes,
will be mountains, islands, plunging cliffs,
or clusters of friends—the Poets of the Bamboo Grove,
perhaps—who made boats of their poems
and floated them out on the river.
There will be no bright colors in my garden.
Evergreens, rather, or moss that has no skin to shed,
for we are talking not of evanescent things
but of the bones and marrow of the world.

Return to the Island
after Wang Wei

I've come home to our northern island,
letting go thoughts of who is in or out.
The white morning sun climbs above
our cottage, dispelling dawn's chill,
rousing thrushes, wrens, waxwings
that dart to our trees and bushes.
I love their chatter and song,
their quick flight, their perfect bodies,
and how branches bend or spring up
as they leave or light.
I cook eggs and boil water for tea.
You ask what laws rule failure or success?
Shouts of children in the orchard
raise a scatter of birds.

FROM
Waiting for the Alchemist
(2009)

Silence at 5 A.M.
Vinalhaven, Maine

Eagles have come back to the island.
Osprey are plentiful again. Soon they will climb
and circle in threes and fours, almost out of sight,
tootling to each other. Last night at dusk a cormorant
burst from its strip of water by the stone bridge.

But where are my morning birds that criss-crossed
our backyard summer after summer?
Finches, gold and purple, black-capped chickadees,
flights of anxious waxwings.
Where is the high, sweet, five-note piccolo call
of the white-throated sparrow?

Orchids and Eagles

Something happened to the cables
that run under miles of water to our island,
so we play cribbage in the light of six candles
and a hurricane lamp.

I look up from my cards. In the black window opposite,
the assortment of candles and the lamp float in the glass,
and I am back in the dining room of a hotel
in Morelia.

Tall white candles and white orchids float in a wall
of wood-framed windows above the valley,
mingled with pricks of light from the old city—
images that have not risen to mind for thirty years.

What is memory? Praise it. Praise its strings and loops
of orchids floating in the night above the old Mexican town—
and yesterday—that pair of eagles, drifting,
floating above the island, dallying with the wind.

Waiting for the Alchemist

The October sun fires late chrysanthemums,
garnet, lavender, bright yellow.
It strikes an antique dollhouse set down
on the stump of an elm.
A wicker bell tolls.

In my back garden at five in the afternoon,
my shadow's a hundred feet long.
If I squint sidewise, just so, at the white sun
on a day like this,
I might discover the philosopher's stone.

The Box of Clouds

I keep a box in my study for things that draw me
and are useful sometimes in adversity.
I keep not one, but three, Indian head pennies,
and old Chinese coins with circlets and squares
cut in their centers. My foot scuffed them up
in an overblown garden.

I keep stamps in odd colors: moss, mauve,
diamond gray. They looked obsolete
the day they were minted.
Feathers that dropped from the sky,
my Airedale's bark, a child's cry.

I keep a fragrance bottle my muse gave me
when I met her in a blue hotel;
and she startled me into remembering
who I am.

Brothers
Peaks Island, Maine

We crept out of bed, pulled on swimsuits
and walked the short distance to the beach.
No one stirred in the houses at Hadlock's Cove.
It was an early Sunday morning in a summer
of world war.

Your plan, hatched at night as the white stroke
of a lighthouse swept the walls of our room,
was to slip into Casco Bay, swim the strait
where deepwater ships ran, to Cushings Island.
I was your ten-year-old accomplice. My task:
to keep silent until the time came for bragging,
row the cold blue mile beside you, and fish you
from the water if you tired or developed a cramp.

We made it clear to Cushings. The Army
kept a coast artillery battery there to smash
any Nazi sub rash enough to shadow our great
gray warships in their roadstead down the bay.

We knew the guns' power. On some mysterious
schedule, they fired from a cliff at targets towed
miles out to sea. The boom cracked windows
on our island.

We hauled the boat up on a beach, walked past
the loading dock. Why not a look around?
Keeping in shadow, we made our way on a path
to a pair of vast metal doors, camouflage green,
carved in the base of a hill.
The doors stood ajar. Where were the guards?

In the gloom of the cave as far as I could see—
rows of artillery shells, each as tall as I was.
You whispered, "Yellow means high explosive."

What if we struck a spark?
The whole east of Cushings would crash into the sea.
What if we got caught?
Loose Lips Sink Ships.

Creeping close to the ground like men
who would soon appear in a thousand war films,
we slipped back to the punt, rowed home,
and never told anybody.

Once in a While

Mother was agitated all morning.
A call had come from her brother Harold,
who was spoken of only in whispers
and despised by those with a talent
for never changing their minds.
But Mother loved him.

Somehow I learned that my uncle
had forged checks and spent time in prison.
And I knew he played the saxophone
in small jazz bands.

In late afternoon the doorbell rang.

My uncle stood in the hall.
A tall man slightly stooped, he shook snow
from his long brown overcoat. He had a high
hooked nose and wavy brown hair
that fell across his forehead,
and he carried packages wrapped in Christmas paper.

My stepfather signaled: disappear.

In early evening Uncle Harold
knocked on my door with a gift for me:
jazz records, the first I'd seen.

Fats Waller beaming from the album cover
is clearer to me now than my uncle's face.
"I can't give you anything but love, baby."

A mourning sax backing Lee Wiley:
"Once in a while, will you give just
one little thought to me . . .

At first light my uncle was gone,
his footprints vanishing in a fresh fall of snow.

The Old Man in the Green House

His house at the edge of the road is tumbledown,
its siding weathered to a noxious shade of green.
The upper windows, stuffed with stained towels,
clatter in a stiff breeze.
Paper plates cover cracks in the glass.

Summer mornings he sits outside in a nine dollar
plastic chair. Even in August heat he wears a sweater.
Such meals as he has he cooks on an old wood stove,
lifting round iron lids to drop the wood inside.

The town has tried to move him to a trim apartment,
one of a small string built for elders.
He won't hear of it.
The social worker has stopped arguing with him.
"He'll starve to death in there," she says,
"if he doesn't burn up in the kitchen fire first."
But most islanders will push just so far.
Then they wonder who is helping whom.

The Dowser

Take this willow fork in your hand.
Hold it in front of you.
Put your thumbs near the tips of the Y
like this. Now walk toward your well.
If you have the gift, the branch will dip
toward the vein of water.

The willow wouldn't stir for me,
but the dowser thought the slow young man
who drifted across the road
and held out his hand for the branch
might be gifted.
Old now, he needed to give
what he knew away.

In the Barbershop

My barber, Franco, has no friends.
"All I do is work, work, work. This is America."
Last fall he closed his shop for a month
and flew to his native town in Catania.

"There I know everybody, they know me.
My wife and I, we walk in the square.
We meet a friend, we sit down, we talk
and have a cappuccino.
Time in Sicily is different from here.
Talk is more important than money.
Do you know the rent I pay for this place?
Where's the leisure, the life?"

All day, as he cuts and shapes
his clients' hair he plays Italian opera.
> *Casta Diva,*
> > *Visi d'arte*
> *Una voce poco fa*
> > *Una furtive lacrima.*

Pavarotti, the great Domingo, Callas, Fleming,
Bartoli. The music surges, shimmers, dies.
Opera is about large emotions.
It melts his confusions, eases his pain.

At George Trambas' Body Shop

My father died when he was 103.
Every day at noon he sat back, drank
a pint of wine, ate fresh tomatoes
from our fields, maybe a piece of fish,
and napped an hour.
When the Nazis came, they smashed
everything. My father pointed to the sky—
"He'll get it back for us."
My mother died at 63.
The Communists shot my brother.
She could not stop grieving.
The picture on the door?
That's me, in a relay race in Athens.
I was 19, strong, quick. I had promise.
The big man with the mustache,
he was my teacher, a champion.
He went to the villages to look
for talented boys. He taught us
to run and throw the discus.
Of ten brothers, I was the one
who came to the States. My son's a dentist,
my daughter works for the county.
I'm 74. How old are you?

I come here six o'clock, six days a week
for twenty years. Too much work.
Too much responsibility.
I called junk yards all over town
for a left front fender. Your car's too old.
But I got one. Maybe they stole it.
I'll try to have the job done by the weekend.
Call me after ten on Friday.
Okay?

The Island Gift Shop
Peaks Island, Maine

In summers long past I walked with my grandfather
from his rooms in Merch's cottage to Harry Coxe's
Island Gift Shop.

I made straight for the shelves made to lure small boys
with lobster traps carved to fit my hand, trawlers,
sailboats, tinny ships in bottles.

He purchased cough drops, butterscotch squares,
the latest Agatha Christie or Ellery Queen.

There were watercolors by the Coxe sisters—
Portland Head Light flashing its beam
to warn of sunken cliffs and ridges—
postcards of the sun slipping down past the brown
ferry dock on Diamond Island, souvenir cushions
packed with cedar and pine.

Here comes Mr. Coxe himself. Tobacco-stained teeth,
sinister laugh, and the sisters, tall and wan in pallid colors.
They leap back, astonishing me, as I walk with you
on another island, and the night wind settles about us
a green cloud of cedar and pine.

The Reading
Adam Zagajewski in Chicago

He was ill at ease at first.
"Can you hear me? This microphone—"
the *o*'s spoken like the French *u*, with pursed lips.
"Is it better now?"
In a voice that rose and fell, half lyric, half ironic,
came poems of a summer dawn streaked
with odors of mint and dark earth,
of swift rivers hesitantly crossed,
crippled towns, refugees dressed for every season
dragging carts behind them.
And poems studded with abstractions
we teach our students to avoid, like
purity, justice, liberty.

My Muse

I walk up to the checkroom
in the dusky lobby of a blue hotel.
The attendant steps in front of her counter.
She holds out a stringed instrument,
its bowl chipped and painted with smudged
red whorls and gold diamonds.

"Don't you recognize me?
Take this, it's yours."
The air about her ripples a bit
and shines.

Your Dream, My Dream

1

In your dream you are walking in a gray
tattered part of the city.
You pause in front of a broken building,
windows gone, twists of graffiti indecipherable
except for the hate, on dirty brown brick.

Somehow you know the phones are alive.
You walk inside and pick up a phone on a desk.
After decades—my voice on the line.

2

In my dream a phone rings past midnight
in a dark office tower.
Another rings far down the hall. And another.
Phones ring all night in empty offices across the city.
Screeds in colorless ink, sparks flying.

Nameless

Every family has them.
Photos of people nobody knows,
distant relatives, perhaps,
friends of parents long dead.

A young man poses under the clock
in Prague's medieval square,
shirt open at the neck.
Why the mocking grin?
Wind ruffles his hair.

Saucy in a filmy blouse
a woman bends toward
her photographer
over emptied coffee cups.
Breasts perky as young trout.
Sun, shadows, an outdoor café.

A family strolls in Karlovy Vary.
Solemn, dark-suited father.
Elegant mother with hat and lace gloves.
She holds a child by the hand,
its head encased in bandages.

Snapshots, nothing remarkable,
but my wife dislikes seeing such photos
framed in shops for sale to strangers.

Last night as dusk settled in, she carried
ours in a box to the back garden
and burned them one by one,
in a kind of funeral.
Inside, she lit a yahrzeit candle.

Song of the Platelets

1

Winter dawn. I raise the shade in my hospital room
above the domes and spires of Chicago. Windy and cold
outside. Steam blowing hard from vents, heeling over
like sails vaporizing away.

My door opens. The masked blood lady.
"Mr. Mark, why you up so early
all the time?"

"I'll need a pressure bandage when you stick me."

"Yes I know. You a bleeder.
Your platelets is so low."

She slaps my arm below the line
of the blue elastic tourniquet
to bring the blood up.

"Now come platelets—be nice.
We need to get this young man
outta this place for New Years.
Talk to your platelets,
Mr. Mark. Talk to them!"

"I'm with you, Benina. I'm with you.
I do talk to my platelets."

2

Second hour after breakfast, the next huge
event of the morning. My attending will arrive
to tell me the result of the platelet exam;
they must reach 10 before I can go home.
He arrives with a smile and a sharp sharp nose.

Interns, residents, thin, short, white coats,
trail and settle after. They are about to perform
a motet outside my room.

"It is *possible*, sir, we may
have to raise the chemo to a somewhat
more aggressive level."

3

In the gray afternoon a retired rabbi, a volunteer
from the chaplain's office, floats by
like an unmoored canoe.

"May I ask, do you
belong to a congregation?"

"I'm sorry, Rabbi, I'm afraid I'm one of those
Jews still unmoored by the Holocaust."

"Personal experience, sir?"

"Not personal, though never remote."

"Rabbi, tell me, who needs a God
who couldn't/wouldn't protect the six million?"

"But Hashem gave man and woman the world,
said do what you're gonna do with it. Hashem,
God the Merciful, God the Judge; both parts of God.
We know what happened. Read the papers, watch TV.
You know the Shema?"

"Hear O Israel, the Lord our God,
the Lord is One."

"I hate to say this to you, Rabbi,"
such a short man, with a smile, a pot belly,

and small gray beard. "I hate to say this:
Even the sublime 23rd is a cop-out, a pipe dream.
I ask myself, do I want it read at my funeral?
It's poetry, not promise."

He will lay a table before me
in the presence of my enemies . . .
In the valley of the Shadow of Death . . .
His Rod, His Staff . . .

4

Night. Not a nurse at the station.
I study the digital clock, tossing off my minutes.

Suddenly, a long-ago attic in the big brick house
my father built above the river and died in soon after.
Somehow, the house is ours again. I am ten.
I open an attic door and walk out under the eaves.
They are there: trunks, dismantled beds, pictures
turned to the wall, toys, games, my lead soldiers.
No one is home. A night of wild wind, violent rain.

But now the murmur of voices
and low bluish lights in the hall.
Things move by on soft wheels.
They have come back, the nurses.
Soon Benina will come to draw blood again.
It must be close to dawn.

I tunnel myself up, almost to the level
of the holy/unholy psalm.

A Late Birthday
for Ted Kooser

Most of what I know
other people learn
at odd moments,
in this kind of silence
or that. But we had
to reach this shore
to find it.

More

I pin a yellow cottonwood leaf
    on my brown cork board
        and that's the fall.

I keep a chunk of an old oak lobster pot
    with rusty nail holes
        and that's the sea.

I have it from a cardinal, the Roman kind,
    diminishment, too,
        is a form of growth.

A Question for Eugène Atget

What is the girl in your celebrated photograph doing?
The organ grinder is grinding away, his mustachios
and cheery dirty face, his instrument, became a cliché
that conjured Paris in a hundred films.
But the girl, her arms thrown in the air—is she crying
or rapturously singing?
How did the morning go for her, when she followed
the old man as he rolled his cart beyond the border
of the picture?

In Memory of My Brother

And so they took your ashes to a quiet cove,
a favorite indent on the wrinkled Maryland coast
along the Miles River, where you would stop
to watch ducks and geese, an osprey hunting,
the shifting calligraphy of the reeds.

In went your ashes, sprinkled over the side
of your handsome day sailor.
Nine grandkids dropped flowers on the water.
One of your sailing buddies, who had tethered
your boat to the others, read *A Mariner's Prayer*,
probably bending your wishes.
Another slid a bottle of double malt scotch
to the muddy bottom.

Champagne all around.
So much for synagogues, churches, bone yards.

Up north where I live, an image of your big blond face
still floats, not among the stars—those cliché machines—
but in daylight over trees and water, over marble clouds.

The Island without Tourists
Vinalhaven, Maine

1

Late September. No more sunsets of lavender,
pale green, rose, soft gray. The west
red-orange like a furnace.

No lights from neighboring houses.
The full moon bright enough to turn the islet
below, each pointed spruce,
upside down in the flat-calm bay.

2

Bright morning. Wind rushes in treetops.
Aerial surf swoops, roughs my hair,
sizzles in my ears.

My own sound in the mix—
big shoes on gravel.
It's all music.

Against Cosmology

I don't care that the universe is fifteen
billion years old.

I don't care that it contains more dark matter
than the leaping zillions of stars,

that there is more empty space
in the universe than anything.

Move close to me. This is our day on Earth
like any other average miraculous day.

In My Next Life

I will own a sailboat sleek
as fingers of wind
and ply the green islands
of the gulf of Maine.
In my next life I will pilot a plane,
and enjoy the light artillery
of the air as I fly to our island
and set down with aplomb
on its grass runway.
I'll be a whiz at math, master five or six
of the world's languages, write poems
strong as Frost and Milosz.
In my next life I won't wonder why
I lie awake from four till daybreak.
I'll be amiable, mostly, but large
and formidable.

I'll insist you be present
in my next life—and the one after that.

The Revelation

I rise in the night and encounter
a strange new scent when I turn
my head just so. At last,
a visit from the other world.

Only Mother would have the fortitude
to travel all that way. And in a pleasant mood,
to judge by the freshness and sweetness
of the scent, to tell me I have long been forgiven
and to learn I long ago forgave her.

I declare an amnesty.
Everyone, everyone is forgiven.

The Kitchen Bird

Above our stove a Persian bird
flies on a Persian tile
in a surround of stalks and flowers,
some blue like his wings,
some like his breast cinnamon-rose.
His beak is open; he stares straight up.
This is the way he greets each morning.
Singing.

NEW POEMS

The Mysteries of Hannah and Ivar

A tall slender man sits at a rolltop desk
in the office of Passage Broker S. Jarmulsky,
32 Canal Street, near the west tower of Brooklyn Bridge.
His name is Ivar, my Swedish grandfather.
He wears a thin brown beard, a mustache, and works
on papers of immigrants like himself, traveling
back and forth from northern Europe.

His eyes are blue as ice on the winter streets
of his native Göteborg.
He has married a woman and sent her away
to live with her parents in far-off Boston.
Times are hard.

Why did Ivar come to this unruly land?

He was traveling with his tutor.
Perhaps the sea air would cure
his migraines.

The trip was a gift from his father
after long university study.

In love with a Christian girl,
he was sent away to thwart their marriage.

Stories, family legends. Each could be true
or not, or some combination, permutation.

He had a gift for languages, he even studied
Aramaic, yet never found a way
to earn a living.

He brought his cane down on the head
of a raw, sunburned man who popped out

from behind a tree in Central Park
and asked for a match.

On days when the black mood seized him
he would brandish that cane in traffic
like Moses at the Red Sea.

Once his mother sent steamship tickets
for the family to visit Sweden.
He burned them in a glass dish
in a kitchen ceremony.

Now from the home of a great-aunt, I receive letters
From Ivar to Hannah in Boston, and from Sweden,
letters from his younger brother Bernhard,
just back from a trip to America.
Both packets tied with brittle ribbons.

Ivar writes in elegant faded script on tea-colored paper.
He complains in graceful English of harried, ten-hour days.
He longs to see his mother and the dustless light of Sweden.
The fear he might lose his job to Jarmulsky's son
sends him to bed with a Migraine (capital letter).
He teases Hannah for being snappish, himself for being cruel.
"You know I am a *very old young man*."
He counsels patience, their separation will end.

Then this—like a slash—from Bernhard,
"I felt such joy when the mail brought your picture,
I kissed it and wept."
He hides the photo from disapproving eyes.

Why did Hannah keep these letters and a small photo
of Bernhard in a box that has gathered silence
for a hundred years?

Had she fallen in love too late with the melancholy smile
of the younger, more ardent brother?

Do I know at last why Ivar burned the steamship tickets,
never returned to Sweden, never saw his family again?

Enough. I weary myself and these subtle ghosts—
and think of what my children
will never know of me.

Poor Willy

He sat on his stoop as we walked to school,
his clothes a washed-out blur of browns and grays.
His head rolled off center, he drooled a little,
his speech a moan.
We called out taunts, thumbed noses,
even hopped and sang.

> *Poor Willy fell in the fire*
> *and was burned to ashes.*
> *All of a sudden the room got chilly.*
> *Someone forgot to poke up Willy.*

Would he hobble after us in a game
of Tortoise and Hare?
Couldn't we bear the sight of so much misery?

What swam at the bottom of our dreams was fear
of the black wind that might rise any time while we slept,
seep under doors, rattle old windows,
and change five boys to toads.

For Jack and Natalie

I saw you yesterday on Michigan Boulevard,
a Friday, at the busiest time of day.
Two old people crossing the boulevard,
a crowd crossing with you, and cars,
cabs and buses cutting in front of you.
Jack, hesitant, tall and dangerously slender,
in an elegant blue jacket, dark trousers.
Black cane.

Natalie, in a fluttering summer dress,
not quite right for a cool May afternoon.
You seemed to be guiding Jack,
And your expression—mouth slightly open,
eyes working hard for both of you—set
between fear and panic.

Did you catch my eye, Natalie;
was there something I might have done?
You were having a day on loud
brassy Michigan Boulevard,
O Jack, O Natalie.

Fresh Linen

The house was yellow with white trim,
the basement white-washed and musty,
with an *Evinrude* or *Johnson Seahorse*
resting in a barrel of water from the tap.
There were thick porcelain washtubs,
spider webs in corners, fishing poles,
carpenter's and garden tools.

There were shade trees in front and flowerbeds:
bright orange nasturtiums, noble peonies, top-heavy
dahlias. Rockers moved in a breeze on the empty porch.
Clothes hung on a rope pulley strung between
a pair of Norway maples.

The sheets rose and billowed in the rinsed light.
They warmed the arms of the boy who unpinned
and took them down.

He carried the breath of a moment in Eden into
the dark wallpapered rooms of the house.

Alexander's Castle

Roaming through my files, I come across
a painting by grandson Alexander.
For me, it is a king's crown, or perhaps
a mountain range, because of the seven
penciled peaks in the background.
You told me a dragon lives there. It has
spiky yellow plates along its spine.
A robot vampire lives there, a turtle,
two boats—splashes of gray, pink and black—
and an elevator.

Alex, when you have forgotten the sound of my voice
and must look far to remember my face,
I hope you will call home the fiery sparks
of your childhood.

To a Helium Balloon Bought at the Zoo for Alex

You presided in our living room for a fortnight
hanging like a harvest moon, large, solemn,
green-eyed, because you could not travel with Alex
on the plane to Denver. Full of yourself at first,
you pressed your orange head hard against the ceiling
and glowered. You made your descent with too much
majesty. Sometimes you displayed your blank silver side,
then turned slowly and stared at me out of tiger eyes,
a mythical judge from elsewhere.
One morning you hung above the mantle. As I stood
unsteady in slippers, you rocked, pivoted,
and we were eye to eye. Today your stare is even
graver. You're missing a certain fullness about the jaws.

Quit wasting time on shows of royalty. Fly after
Alex. Image for him grace and buoyancy. Teach him
daring and staying power and to remember in perilous
times to keep something of himself for himself.
Let him know what a grand run it was in the forest
when you were full of phizz.

An Afternoon with Bill Stafford

An unsettling man, who said anyone can be a poet.
Simply, push off on the river of your life,
that stream that is always there, no matter
what happens in Boston or Bangladesh.
Your boat scrapes against the bank? Put that in.
You knock against a stone bridge? Put that down.
But keep trolling, trolling in the current
of your own dark song.

The Hidden Pool
for Trudy Paddock

In a box marked Priority
delivered to the door,
a pastel by a friend.
Brushes and paints
are a struggle for her to wield.

Penciled on the back
in her spidery hand:
Hidden Pool, Vinalhaven,
Dushane Quarry, 2004.

The water a deeper blue than I remember,
with odd flecks of orange and crimson,
brown rocks folded by the glacier
and colors mined from within
as if glimpsed beyond the world's rim.

The Beam

Carved in warm gray stone
        a Japanese monk
              stands
in a busy hall of the museum
long-fingered hands
        pressed together
eyes shut in their large sockets
        the beam of a smile
              travels inward
                      silence
in the long folds of his robe

A Late Watercolor by Cézanne

A few green and blue touches
    almost transparent
coalesce into tall trees, water,
    and a force
I cannot see or name.

At the Basil Leaf Café

When I, old explorer, look at this young woman
seated in the restaurant against the light of a gray
November day—her magenta blouse, her bright green
vest, and tan fedora pushed back stylishly, and her baby
at her side in its stroller—I think of her in a role
she cannot imagine: she is holding up the sky for all of us.

AFTERWORD

During his lifetime, Mark Perlberg published four collections of poems (*The Burning Field*, 1970; *The Feel of the Sun*, 1981; *The Impossible Toystore*, 2000; and *Waiting for the Alchemist*, 2009). During the last year of his life, he told me that he wished some of his early poems, then out of print, might appear in book form once more, together with his later work. He began to re-read his poems, selecting those he thought worthy of a second appearance in print. This became his final project, one he discussed with me often and in detail. After his death, I found his notes and decided to complete the project to his specifications.

Together with the new, previously unpublished work, these poems are recollections and meditations on the whole of his life experience—family mythology, his father's early death, the role of art, the nature of childhood, the individual in the moment, confrontation with illness, the nuances of the natural world, the complexity of love. The subjects are often explored through the eyes of random characters—fellow poets, historical figures, eccentric neighbors, struggling immigrants, his grandparents and grandchildren. The reader is transported to multiple settings, most frequently the rocky, pungent coast of Maine, site of our summer home on the island of Vinalhaven.

To his task of storytelling Mark brings a keen awareness of the pleasures of the senses, together with a subtle responsiveness to his natural surroundings—the play of light and shadow, the ocean splashing on rocks, the flight of birds. Marked by clarity of vision, purity of language, and depth of feeling, the collection is, in effect, a memoir, articulated in the voice of the lyric poet. The voice is unmistakably his own.

The trajectory of Mark's life took him from beginnings in New York and New Jersey, and formative summers on Peaks Island, Maine, to education at Hobart College and Columbia University, where we met as fellow students. We were married during the Korean War, and then spent two years in the Far East—an experience that greatly influenced his development as an artist. After returning to the United States, we moved to Chicago, where our two daughters were born.

Chicago was Mark's home base for the rest of his life—a life that was rich with work as reporter and editor, participation as an activist in local politics, and many trips abroad. Together with other Chicago poets, he founded The Poetry Center of Chicago in the seventies, and served as its president for several years. This institution invited leading writers of the United States, as well as the outside world, to read their work and engage with Chicago audiences.

Supporting his family as a journalist, Mark wrote his poems between assignments, during long nights, on vacation trips. A few of the final poems in this collection were written at the Lannan Foundation's writers' colony in Marfa, Texas. Mark was active and writing until his death in 2008. His final poem, "Song of the Platelets," was written as he was dying in the hospital.

The completion of Mark's final project was a difficult though rewarding task for me. When I had finished assembling and arranging the collection as I believe he intended, his publisher, Louisiana State University Press, generously agreed to publish it as his final work. The result is the present volume, the valedictory memoir of a poet.

Anna Nessy Perlberg

www.ingramcontent.com/pod-product-compliance
Lightning Source LLC
Chambersburg PA
CBHW031633160426
43196CB00006B/391